— THE FLOUR POT —

# Cookie Book

## CREATING EDIBLE WORKS OF ART

*Margie and Abbey Greenberg*

RUNNING PRESS

PHILADELPHIA · LONDON

9 8 7 6 5 4 3 2 1
Digit on the right indicates the number of this printing

Library of Congress Control Number: 2005929945

ISBN-13: 978-0-7624-2595-2
ISBN-10: 0-7624-2595-4

Photographs by Steve Legato
Cover and Interior design by Alicia Freile
Edited by Diana von Glahn
Typography: Bellevue, Futura, and Bell MT

This book may be ordered by mail from the publisher.
Please include $2.50 for postage and handling.
*But try your bookstore first!*

Running Press Book Publishers
125 South Twenty-second Street
Philadelphia, Pennsylvania 19103-4399

Visit us on the web!
www.runningpress.com

To the bond between Mothers and Daughters.

# Contents

Thank you Freddie (Dad), for truly believing in our cookies, our ideas, and us.
We love you.

Thank you Andy, for the late night phone calls and never tiring of discussions
on our greater vision.

Thank you Ira, for your support, both technical and personal.
And for understanding about family business. You're our number one taste tester.

Thank you Shiri, for allowing the kids to eat dessert first.

Thank you Hallie, for painting The Flour Pot kitchen pink.

Thank you Sara, for always wanting to hold the bag of cookies.

Thank you Pop Pop and Grandmom, for anxiously awaiting broken cookies.

Thank you to The Flour Pot staff who rally to all occasions and are the bones of
our operation. And especially to Karen who fills our little kitchen with big smiles.
And to Doris, the best dough-roller we know.

Thank you Diana and Running Press, for giving us this fabulous opportunity.

———◆◆◆———

And thank you to the Flour Pot customers, especially those who trusted us to be
creative when we first started. Thank you for loving what we love to make. Enjoy!

# Introduction

**Abbey** Cookie decorating has the ability to breathe life into your most creative fantasies. One cookie will transport you to a beach chair in the south of France, while another might take you to the side of a frozen lake, old fashioned ice skates in hand. You can be the designer of *haute couture* or a little kid in a candy shop. After enjoying the many places cookie decorating has brought us, we wanted to create this book to enable you to let your imagination take you to fabulous places!

**Margie** Most of the cookies that we make are favors to be enjoyed on a special occasion. Each cookie is a special package given away to celebrate the day's event. That's why our cookies have a look of festivity. They virtually demand a party or celebration! The palette of most of our cookies is also festive because we like to use lots of bright colors.

**Abbey** Customers always ask us how our icing edges are so neat and clean. It's simple! We decorate our cookies with fondant that is cut with a cookie cutter! No mess, no runny edges, no piping necessary! Fondant as the first layer of icing on our cookies provides a wonderfully soft texture before the sugar cookie. But fondant is very sweet, so the covering for a cookie must be very thin.

**Margie** I fell in love with fondant during my first cake decorating class in New York. It is a popular sweet icing for special occasion cakes. The finish is smooth and very adaptable. It is very easy to dye, enabling you to make it any color you choose, or a combination of colors.

**Abbey** At one of our workshops, someone asked, "How do you know if the colors match?" We say, it doesn't matter! Don't be afraid of color here. Whatever colors you use, just stick to similar tones (brights with brights, pastels with pastels, jewel tones with jewel tones). The rest will fall into place. We've suggested colors throughout this book, but feel free to use whatever colors suit your fancy. The sky's the limit with cookie decorating!

**Margie** I don't think you ever have to match colors! They all seem to work together—and the oddest colors paired up often make the most exciting end result.

Seasons also dictate our choice of colors. We are more likely to use jewel tones for autumn themed cookies, cool icy tones (plus green and red) for winter themed cookies, pastels for the spring, and hot, bright colors for the summer.

I think my favorite part of decorating the cookies is adding the accessories—a bow, a flower, dragées—whatever! Abbey likes the cookies a bit less fussy but I say the more the better!

**Abbey** My childhood was filled with parties, not because I was a social butterfly, but because my mom was a professional party decorator. While she arranged parties from start to finish, I was in the background pretending that I, too, was turning a bare room into a wonderland of theme and magic.

I suppose it's no surprise that I have been influenced by some of my mom's rules of party planning. Even my very first attempt at entertaining—a housewarming party my sophomore year of college—had a theme. I think the most important lesson that I've learned about entertaining and party planning is that a party is made in the details. Every detail counts and each detail can make a party that much better.

So, it comes as no surprise that those lessons have transferred into what we do today. Every detail counts. The addition of one more ribbon, or one more dragée can turn a simple cookie into a work of art.

In *The Flour Pot Cookie Book*, we invite you to learn how to make our decorative cookies, a cookie party if you will, where a work of art is but a detail away. Enjoy!

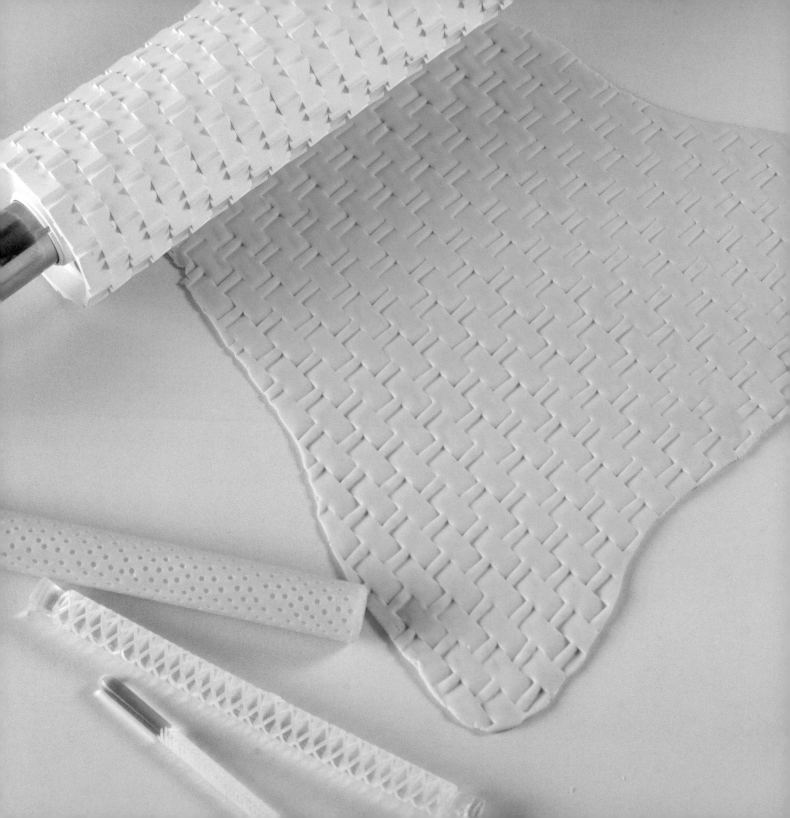

# Basic Tools

- Rolling pin

- Cookie sheets

- Cookie cutters

- Fondant: For each 4-inch cookie, you need about 1 ounce of fondant

- Fondant rolling pin (plain and textured)

- Parchment paper

- Paintbrushes

- Corn syrup

- Pastry bags

- Pastry bag tips

- Colored gel paste

- Latex gloves

- Toothpicks

- Decorative accessories: We call anything that is not the first layer of fondant an accessory! We accessorize our cookies like some people accessorize with a scarf or belt. While plainly decorated cookies are pretty, we think they are oh so much prettier all decked out! We think you can never have too many accessories!

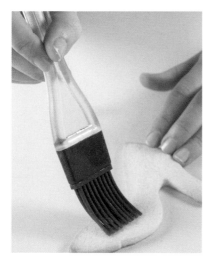

*Brushing corn syrup adhesive on cookie.*

*Cutting fondant with cookie cutter.*

*Brushing Luster Dust as a final touch.*

# GARDEN PARTY

# Daisies

*The classic daisy shape is a wonderful starter cookie. Its simple shape provides a good canvas to practice and perfect the steady rhythmic hand that is key to good piping.*

---

This is one of our most requested cookies. The daisies are bright and cheerful. It's a basic cookie and a great place to start for beginners. We like these hot colors because they remind us of a summer garden. Use whatever colors suit your mood!

## WHAT YOU NEED:

Fondant rolling pin
Colored fondant
Parchment paper
Daisy cookie cutter
Paintbrush
Corn syrup
Daisy cookie
Pastry bag with #2 tip
White royal icing
Candy

## DIRECTIONS:

Roll the fondant on parchment paper until it is ⅛-inch thick. Cut it with your cookie cutter. Use a paintbrush to dab corn syrup on the top of your cookie. Carefully place fondant on the cookie, smoothing the edges with a dry finger.

Outline the petals of your flower with royal icing.

Adhere the candy to the center of your daisy with royal icing.

Let dry for at least one hour or until the fondant is hardened.

*Another idea:* The center of your daisy can be as large or as small as you like. Sometimes, we use a small candy for the center, and other times, we use a large fondant circle and pipe royal icing dots on that. Our favorite daisy center is a nonpareil candy—the larger the better! We like the texture of the white, seed-like candies covering the chocolate disc. The contrast in textures also gives the cookie a nice dimension.

---

*Remember:* For easier handling, warm fondant in your hands for a minute or two before rolling it out.

---

● **Abbey says:** This the first cookie I learned to pipe.

● **Margie says:** I was at a party when one of the guests brought a box of handmade nonpareils. They were the size of silver dollars and had a wonderful dark chocolate flavor! If I had my choice, these would always be the centers of my daisies.

# Ladybugs

*These ladybug cookies look fabulous when grouped together, but are also delightfully whimsical when placed in and around a dessert table—just like little good luck treats!*

———◆◆◆———

**Ladybugs bring good luck—especially if one lands on you. We love the idea of lucky cookies! A little color surprise is fun. We like to throw in a green ladybug into the mix every now and again.**

## WHAT YOU NEED:

Fondant rolling pin
Red fondant
Parchment paper
Ladybug cookie cutter
Paintbrush
Corn syrup
Ladybug cookie
Black royal icing
Pastry bag with #2 tip
White royal icing

## DIRECTIONS:

Roll fondant on parchment paper until it is ⅛-inch thick. Cut it with your cookie cutter. Use a paintbrush to dab corn syrup on the top of your cookie. Carefully place fondant on the cookie, smoothing the edges with a dry finger.

With black royal icing in your pastry bag, pipe an outline of the head of your ladybug. Fill in the outline with black icing until no red fondant shows through. Pipe a line down the middle of your ladybug, starting at the head and going all the way to the bottom. Pipe dots on either side of this line.

Using a new pastry bag filled with white royal icing (or you can wash out the black icing from the first bag), pipe two dots for eyes on the ladybug's head.

Let dry for at least one hour or until the fondant is hardened.

*Another idea:* If you are not comfortable piping, use small, circular cookie cutters (or the small end of a piping tip) to cut out black fondant circles. Adhere these to your ladybug with corn syrup.

*Remember: When piping dots onto your cookie, be sure to hold the pastry bag for a few seconds while piping to create a plump dot.*

●**Abbey says:** This cookie design is one of my mom's favorites.

# Silverware

*Perfect for ladies who want a dainty treat with their coffee or tea. And what a wonderful way to show guests your knack for all things extraordinary!*

---•◆•---

These silverware cookies are a nice accent to any dessert tray. They are also wonderful treats for an afternoon tea or a shower brunch. Change the colors of the ribbons and fondant to match your event.

## WHAT YOU NEED:

Fondant rolling pin
Pink fondant
Parchment paper
Silverware cookie cutters
Small knife
2 Paintbrushes
Corn syrup
Silverware cookies
Scoring tool (or toothpick)
White fondant
Super Pearl Luster Dust
White royal icing
Pastry bag with #2 tip
Ribbon bow
Dragées (optional)

## DIRECTIONS:

Roll pink fondant on parchment paper until it is $\frac{1}{8}$-inch thick. Cut it with the cookie cutter. Use a knife to separate the top of the fondant utensil from its handle or base. Save the fondant from the top for later use. Use a paintbrush to dab corn syrup on the handle of your cookie. Carefully place the fondant piece on your cookie, smoothing the edges with a dry finger. While the fondant is still soft, use a scoring tool to score lines on the fondant. Be careful not to press too hard or you will cut right through the fondant.

Roll white fondant until it is $\frac{1}{8}$-inch thick. Cut with your cookie cutter. Use a knife to separate the top of your fondant utensil from its handle or base. Save the base fondant for later use. Dab corn syrup on the head of your cookie. Carefully place the fondant on the head of your cookie, smoothing the edges with a dry finger.

With the unused paintbrush, brush Super Pearl Luster Dust on your cookie. Be sure to do this when the fondant is still soft.

Adhere ribbon and dragées on your cookie using royal icing as glue.

Let dry for at least one hour or until the fondant is hardened.

---

***Remember:*** *It's only a cookie! If you do not like your decorating, someone else will still love eating it!*

---

# Teapot

*When you're setting the table for afternoon tea or a garden party, it is fun to mix and match different china patterns—and it's equally fun to do this with cookies.*

◦—◉—◦

The lids on these teapots are a little askew, but this adds a bit of whimsy to the cookie design. For these cookies, we chose a light color for the base so the darker colored accents would really pop.

## WHAT YOU NEED:

Fondant rolling pin

Fondant – 2 colors

Parchment paper

Textured fondant rolling pin

Small flower cookie cutter

Teapot cookie cutter

Half-moon cookie cutter

Knife

Paintbrush

Corn syrup

Teapot cookie

Sugar flowers

White royal icing

Pastry bag with #2 tip

## DIRECTIONS:

Roll base fondant on parchment paper until it is ⅛-inch thick. Roll the textured rolling pin once over the fondant. Set aside.

Roll out the colored fondant you will be using as accent to ⅛-inch thickness. Cut out a few flowers using the small flower cookie cutter. Place these cut outs on the base fondant. Using a different color fondant, make tiny balls and place these in the center of each fondant flower. Roll this out until everything is flat.

Cut the fondant with the teapot cookie cutter and use the half-moon cutter to create the handle.

With a paintbrush, dab corn syrup on the top of your cookie. Carefully place the fondant on the cookie and smooth with a dry finger.

Adhere sugar flowers with royal icing. Accent the teapot with dots and swirls of white icing.

Let dry for at least one hour or until the fondant is hardened.

*Remember: Adding accent fondant to your base fondant can result in wasted fondant; rolling and re-rolling fondant with too many colors mixed in will eventually turn brown or an unappealing color. Try to create patterns in small portions or stick to colors that blend well (like green and yellow). You can also use colors that create other nice colors, like red and blue (purple) or pink and orange (peach). Sometimes, we stumble upon a color we love and can't remember how we made it!*

● **Margie says:** I used to collect Antique English chintz ware, so when I think of teapots, I think of an English garden and floral patterns.

YOU'RE INVITED!

# Clown on a Stick

*What could be more perfect for a child's birthday party than these cookies?!*
*The kids eat these like lollipops. They're great for a circus or carnival themed celebration.*

**WHAT YOU NEED:**

Parchment paper
White fondant
Fondant rolling pin
Clown cookie cutter
Knife
Paintbrush
Corn syrup
Clown cookie on a stick
Colored fondant
Pastry bags
#2 tip
Orange royal icing
White royal icing
Candies
Red royal icing
Black royal icing
Blue royal icing
#18 star tip
Ribbons

Roll white fondant on parchment paper until it is ⅛-inch thick. Use your cookie cutter to cut the fondant. With a knife, cut just below the hat. You'll only be using the clown's white face. Dab the face of your clown cookie with corn syrup. Carefully place the fondant on the cookie and smooth the edges with a dry finger.

Roll an accent fondant until it is ⅛-inch thick. Make pea-sized balls of other accent colors and place them on the rolled accent fondant. Roll the fondant again until all of the balls are flat. Cut with the cookie cutter and trim off the hat. Dab the hat of your cookie with corn syrup and carefully place the fondant hat, smoothing the edges with your finger.

Since you'll be using a variety of royal icing colors here, make your colored icings and fill the bags all at once, so they're ready for use.

Pipe orange royal icing hair where the hat meets the face. Pipe white royal icing mouth and eyes. Adhere candies on your clown's nose and hat. Pipe cheeks and mouth with red royal icing. Pipe black royal icing dots on top of the white eyes.

With blue royal icing in your pastry bag and an #18 star tip, pipe stars along the bottom of the clown's hat, just above his hair.

Wrap the stick and the base of the cookie with ribbons.

Let dry for at least one hour or until the fondant is hardened.

*Another idea:* These cookies and other cookies on a stick look great when propped in popcorn or other decorative boxes. You can find them at any a party supply store. Put a weight in the bottom of the box and fill with popcorn. Place the stick of your cookie in the box, almost like a floral arrangement. This makes a great centerpiece and party favor in one!

● **Abbey says:** Decorating clown cookies is a great activity to do with kids. My nieces Hallie and Sara love to be in charge of the clown's candy hat.
● **Margie says:** Give your clowns different personalities by piping different faces on them.

# Balloons

*This is a great basic cookie. The wow factor is the sparkle,*
*which is a simple finishing touch added at the end.*

**WHAT YOU NEED:**

Parchment paper
Fondant rolling pin
Colored fondant
Balloon cookie cutter
Two paintbrushes
Corn syrup
Balloon cookies
Super Pearl Luster Dust
Ribbons (optional)

**DIRECTIONS:**

Roll fondant on parchment paper until it is ⅛-inch thick. Use your balloon cookie cutter to cut the fondant. Paint the top of a cookie with corn syrup. Carefully place the fondant on top of the cookie and smooth the edges with a dry finger.

Dip the other paintbrush into the Super Pearl Luster Dust and shake off the excess. Paint the fondant with the dust.

Let dry for at least one hour or until the fondant is hardened.

Tie ribbons to the base of each cookie.

*Another idea:* Try making patterns on your cookies or use royal icing to write the birthday boy or girl's age.

*Remember: Paint Luster Dust on your fondant when the fondant is still soft, it will adhere better.*

# Party Hats

*It's a party on a hat! Or as we call it, a self-contained party.*

---

**WHAT YOU NEED:**

Parchment paper

Fondant—2 colors

Fondant rolling pin

Textured fondant rolling pin

Party hat cookie cutter

Paintbrush

Corn syrup

Party hat cookie

Border cutter

#2 Pastry tip

Toothpick

Pastry bag

White royal icing

Colored royal icing

Ribbons or sugar flowers

Candies or cereal

**DIRECTIONS:**

Roll fondant on parchment paper until it is ⅛-inch thick. Go over once with the textured rolling pin. Use your cookie cutter to cut the fondant. Trim off the top, pom pom shaped part of your fondant hat and save for later use. Paint the top of a cookie with corn syrup, avoiding the pom pom part. Carefully place the fondant on top of the cookie, and smooth the edges with a dry finger.

Roll the accent fondant until it is ⅛-inch thick. Use a border cutter to cut a ¾-inch wide strip of fondant. Cut the strip so it fits the bottom of your hat. Using the tip of your #2 pastry tip, create the look of lace by poking small holes in your accent trim. Use a toothpick to clean the fondant out of the tip.

Adhere the lace trim to the bottom of your cookie with royal icing.

Pipe colored royal icing onto the pom pom part of your cookie. Loop ribbons or sugar flowers and adhere them to the royal icing. Add a little more icing and adhere candy to the center of the ribbon.

Let dry for at least one hour or until the fondant is hardened.

*Another idea:* If you don't have candy on hand, use colorful cereal. You can also adhere a bow to your hat's trim for a really decked out hat!

---

**Remember:** *Your local craft and party goods stores have a great selection of festive ribbons and wrapping to decorate your cookies.*

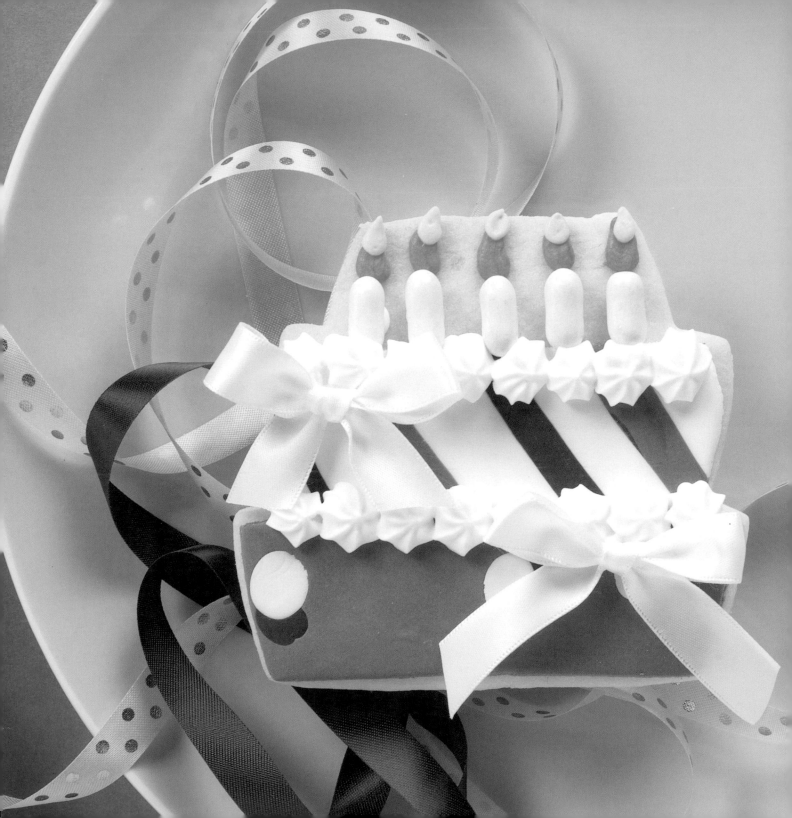

# Birthday Cake

*Birthday cakes are great at any age. Here, we used a more sophisticated color palette for a more sophisticated birthday boy or girl.*

---

**WHAT YOU NEED:**

White fondant
Chocolate fondant
Fondant rolling pin
Parchment paper
Cake cookie cutter
Knife
Paintbrush
Corn syrup
Cake cookie
White royal icing
Pastry bag with #2 tip
Ribbons & candies (optional)

*Remember: Chocolate fondant has a chocolate flavor and different consistency than regular fondant. It's more difficult to roll because it can be sticky. If this happens, add a bit of cocoa powder. This should dry it out a bit.*

**DIRECTIONS:**

Mix some of the white fondant with some of the chocolate fondant to create a mocha-colored fondant. Roll the fondant on parchment paper until it is ⅛-inch thick. Make pea-sized balls of white and chocolate fondant and place them on the rolled fondant. Roll the fondant out again until the balls are incorporated into the fondant. To create stripes, place thin ropes onto the fondant and roll out.

Use your cookie cutter to cut the fondant. With a knife, separate the bottom tier of the cake from the top tier. Set aside the top layer but do not discard; it can be the top for another cookie.

Use a paintbrush to dab corn syrup onto the bottom tier of your cookie. Carefully place fondant on the cookie, smoothing the edges with a dry finger.

Roll out a piece of white fondant. Make a pattern of stripes and dots with chocolate fondant. Roll out the fondant to ⅛-inch thickness and cut out with the cookie cutter. Separate tiers as before, setting aside the bottom for another cookie.

Dab corn syrup on the top tier of the cookie and gently place fondant on the cookie. Don't worry if the pieces don't sit next to each other exactly.

Pipe royal icing accents between the layers of the cake. Use it as glue to adhere decorations to your cookies.

Let dry for at least one hour or until the fondant is hardened.

*Another idea:* Use Good & Plenty® candies for candles. Or pipe candles onto your cake cookies using royal icing. We like to use candies because they add dimension. Don't forget the flame!

Create plaid patterns by laying fondant ropes on top of each other and rolling them out.

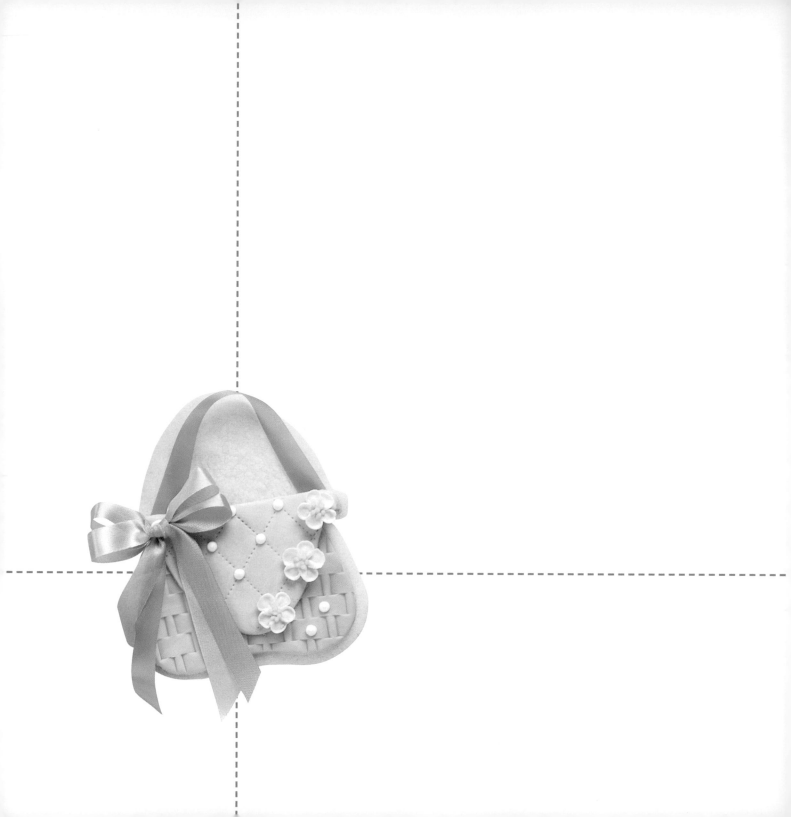

OH SO STYLISH!

- - - - - - - - - - - - - - - - - - - - - - - - - - - - - - - - - - - - - - - - - - - - - - - - - - - - - - - - - - - - - - - - - - - - - - - - - - - - - - - - - - - - - - - - -

# Shoes

*Inspired by the painfully sexy yet gorgeous shoes models wear on the runway, these high fashion designs are easier to create than they are to walk in!*

———— ✦ ————

Our fashion cookies are the collection that started our company. We were asked to create shoes, hats, and pocketbooks for a fashion show for the charity "From the Heart." They are still our most popular and most requested cookies.

## WHAT YOU NEED:

Fondant rolling pin
Fondant—2 colors
Parchment paper
Textured fondant rolling pin
Shoe cookie cutter
Paintbrush
Corn syrup
Shoe cookie
Pastry bag with #2 tip
Royal icing
Ribbons

## DIRECTIONS:

Roll base fondant on parchment paper until it is ⅛-inch thick. Add the accent fondant in whatever pattern you like and roll into the fondant. Roll over the fondant once with the textured rolling pin. Cut the fondant with the shoe cookie cutter.

Use a paintbrush to dab corn syrup on the top of your cookie. Carefully place fondant on the cookie, smoothing the edges with a dry finger.

Pipe royal icing details on your shoe. Adhere ribbon to shoe with royal icing.

Let dry for at least one hour or until the fondant is hardened.

*Another idea:* Use small cookie cutters, a tracing wheel, or a sharp knife to create a variety of designs to adorn your shoe. Or, cut off part of the toe to create an open toe look.

# Hats

*Abbey says: For as long as I can remember, my mom has loved collecting hats—the fussier the better. She even went so far as to host a mother-daughter tea party, requiring all the guests to don a hat! I think she feels that hats are a nod to an era gone by.*

Tulle adds dimension and a sense of drama and glamour to your hats. Try some cookies with and without and see which you prefer. But remember, if you use tulle, don't eat the cookie (without removing the tulle, that is!).

## WHAT YOU NEED:

Fondant rolling pin
White fondant
Parchment paper
Fondant—2 colors
Hat cookie cutter
Paintbrush
Corn syrup
Hat cookie
Textured fondant rolling pin
Knife
Ribbons
Pastry bag with #2 tip
White or other color royal icing
Tulle (optional)

## DIRECTIONS:

Roll fondant on parchment paper until it is ⅛-inch thick. Make small pea-sized balls of accent fondant and place on base fondant. Roll until flat. Cut it with your cookie cutter. Use a paintbrush to dab corn syrup on the top of your cookie. Carefully place fondant on the cookie, smoothing the edges with a dry finger.

Roll accent fondant until it is ⅛-inch thick. Roll it once with a textured rolling pin. Trim off the top half of the hat and discard the bottom. Dab corn syrup on the top half of the cookie and carefully place fondant. Smooth edges with finger.

For hat accents: Take three colors of fondant and roll thin ropes of each. Combine the ropes by twisting them together into one rope. Adhere the rope with royal icing to the center of your hat, where the two fondants meet. Trim excess rope off edge of cookie.

You can also adhere sugar flowers or ribbon, or a combination (see photo).

Pipe white royal icing detail and dots on your hat. Adhere a ribbon bow to the hat with royal icing.

Let dry for at least one hour or until the fondant is hardened.

*Another idea:* To create a ruffled edge, while the fondant is soft, use your fingers to pinch up the edges of the fondant. Hold until firm.

**Remember:** *You can always make less complicated decorations on your cookies, just use less fondant or decorations.*

# Pocketbooks

*Unleash your inner designer! Each fashion design is one of a kind
and truly a work of art. Have fun with your designs and color palette.
Remember: fashion is daring!*

———— ◆ ————

**Believe it or not, the less the colors match, the better these cookies look!**

**WHAT YOU NEED:**

Parchment paper
Fondant—2 colors
Fondant rolling pin
Textured fondant rolling pin
Pocketbook cookie cutter
Knife
Paintbrush
Corn syrup
Pocketbook cookie
Ribbon
Pasty bag with a #2 tip
White royal icing
Tracing wheel (found in sewing stores)
Sugar flowers

**DIRECTIONS:**

Roll fondant on parchment paper until it is ⅛-inch thick. Go over once with the textured rolling pin. Use your pocketbook cookie cutter to cut the fondant. Trim off the top of the pocketbook and save for later use.

Adhere the ribbon handle to the cookie with corn syrup.

Paint the bottom part of your pocketbook cookie with corn syrup. Carefully place the fondant on the cookie and smooth the edges with a dry finger.

Roll accent color until it is ⅛-inch thick. Cut with cookie cutter. Trim the top of the pocketbook with a knife and save the bottom for later use. Turn the top of the pocketbook cut out upside down and adhere it with corn syrup to the top of the pocketbook bottom, so it becomes the pocketbook flap.

While the fondant flap is still soft, make a criss-cross pattern resembling stitching lines on it with the tracing wheel.

Pipe royal icing detail on your pocketbook and use it to adhere ribbons and sugar flowers.

Let dry for at least one hour or until the fondant is hardened.

● **Abbey says:** These cookies got us started. They will always be my favorite, aesthetically and sentimentally.

# Martini and Olives

*We were asked to create these for a customer's Sex and the City season finale party.*
*We think they are chic cookies for any chic celebration!*

Fondant rolling pin
White fondant
Parchment paper
Martini cookie cutter
Paintbrush
Corn syrup
Martini cookie
Olive fondant
Small oval cutter
Toothpick
Pastry bag with #2 tip
White royal icing
Red royal icing
Large oval cookie cutter
Large oval cookie

**DIRECTIONS:**

Roll white fondant on parchment paper until it is ⅛-inch thick. Cut it with your martini cookie cutter. Use a paintbrush to dab corn syrup on the top of your cookie. Carefully place fondant on the cookie, smoothing the edges with a dry finger.

Roll olive fondant until it is ⅛-inch thick. Use a small oval cutter to cut out an olive. Lightly indent the edge of the olive with the oval cutter. Adhere the toothpick to the cookie with white royal icing. Place fondant olive on toothpick.

Pipe a large dot of red royal icing as a pimento. Detail the outside of your martini glass with white royal icing.

Let dry for at least one hour or until the fondant is hardened.

For the large olive:

Roll olive fondant until it is ⅛-inch thick. Cut with large oval cutter. Use a paintbrush to dab corn syrup on the top of your cookie. Carefully place fondant on the cookie, smoothing the edges with a dry finger. Use small cutter to lightly indent the top of the olive. Do not press all the way.

Pipe red royal icing to create pimento.

Let dry for at least one hour or until the fondant is hardened.

*Another idea:* Make a cookie martini bar! Use colored fondant instead of white to create a fruitini and substitute the olive for a strawberry or another fruit.

***Remember:*** *Decorated cookies are great for parties. For more formal sit down parties, consider an assortment of favors. The "ooh-ahh" factor goes a long way as a conversation piece. For more casual parties, put your cookies in a basket to hand out to your guests as parting gifts.*

I DO! I DO!

# Hand with Ring

*What newly-engaged girl wouldn't love this cookie?!!*

------◆------

This cookie is great for engagement parties or bridal showers.

**WHAT YOU NEED:**

Parchment paper
White fondant
Fondant rolling pin
Hand cookie cutter
Paintbrush
Corn syrup
Hand cookie
Border cutter
#2 tip
Toothpick
Pastry bag
White royal icing
Ribbons
Dragées

**DIRECTIONS:**

Roll fondant on parchment paper until it is ⅛-inch thick. Cut it with your cookie cutter. Use a paintbrush to dab corn syrup on the top of your cookie. Carefully place fondant on the cookie, smoothing the edges with a dry finger.

Roll more white fondant until it is ⅛-inch thick and cut a strip about ½-inch wide with border cutter. This will be a decorative cuff on your hand. Use the end of your #2 pastry tip to poke small holes in the strip, creating a lace-like design. Clean out your tip with a toothpick.

Pipe white royal icing at the cookie's cuff and carefully place this fondant onto the cookie. Adhere a bow to the trim's corner with royal icing.

Adhere dragées to hand's ring finger with royal icing.

Let dry for at least one hour or until the fondant is hardened.

*Another idea:* Use colored royal icing as nail polish for your cookie hand! Just pipe it on like you're painting nails.

*Remember: Decorative cookies are thoughtful tokens of thanks for party guests. They are handmade, one of a kind, and delicious. These cookies are great for bridal showers.*

# Bridal Hat

*The wow factor in these cookies comes from not only the attention to detail, but also from the sheer art of cookie decorating.*

---

**WHAT YOU NEED:**

Fondant rolling pin
White fondant
Parchment paper
Hat cookie cutter
Textured fondant rolling pin
Paintbrush
Corn syrup
Hat cookie
Pastry bag with #2 tip
White royal icing
Tulle (optional)
Sugared rose

**DIRECTIONS:**

Roll fondant on parchment paper until it is ⅛-inch thick. Cut it with your cookie cutter. Go over it once with a textured rolling pin. Use a paintbrush to dab corn syrup on the top of your cookie. Carefully place fondant on the cookie, smoothing the edges with a dry finger.

Pipe white royal icing detail and dots on your hat. Gather tulle and adhere to the hat with royal icing. Adhere a sugared rose in the center of the tulle. Pipe dots along the veil.

Let dry for at least one hour or until the fondant is hardened.

*Another idea:* To create a ruffled edge, while the fondant is soft, use your fingers to pinch up the edges of the fondant. Hold until firm.

You can also create a design along your hat's brim by adhering flowers.

---

***Remember:*** *You can always make less complicated decorations on your cookies, just use less fondant or decorations. Here, you can make the hat without a veil and it's just as nice.*

---

# Wedding Cake

*These cookies are truly a gift that any bride or bride-to-be will adore and cherish.*

---

Layers and clusters of flowers adorn this well-dressed cookie for a special wedding.

## WHAT YOU NEED:

Parchment paper
Colored fondant
Fondant rolling pin
Paintbrush
Corn syrup
Tiered Cake cookie cutter
Tiered Cake cookie
Pastry bag with #2 tip
White royal icing
Ribbons
Sugar flowers and sugar flower buds
Green fondant
Leaf stamp

## DIRECTIONS:

Roll base fondant on parchment paper until it is ⅛-inch thick. Use your cookie cutter to cut the fondant. Paint your cookie with corn syrup. Carefully place the fondant on the cookie and smooth the edges with a dry finger.

Roll green fondant to ⅛-inch thick. Use a leaf stamp to make leaves and set them aside to dry. Arrange flowers, buds, and leaves on cake. Once you're happy with their location, adhere them to the cake with royal icing.

Pipe royal icing in the center of the flowers and detail with small royal icing dots.

Let dry for at least one hour or until the fondant is hardened.

---

**Remember:** *Keep an open mind when finding decorations for your cookies. Many of these flowers were broken, but they work perfectly well poking in and around the other flowers and leaves.*

---

● **Abbey says:** My mom's years as party decorator inspired this cookie. I used to watch her arrange floral centerpieces—each flower and decoration was placed with specific intention. Watching her decorate this cookie made me think of that time.

# Couture Bridal Gown

*Be it lace or dragées, handmade flowers or textured ribbons, the possibilities are endless when creating a couture cookie. As with all of our cookies, there is no right or wrong. If you love lace, add it! If you love sugar pearls, have a ball!*

---

**Haute couture** inspired this detailed cookie, with its layers of fondant and fabric.
Experiment with different materials, but be sure to remove them before you eat the cookie!

## WHAT YOU NEED:

Fondant rolling pin
White fondant
Parchment paper
Dress cookie cutter
Textured fondant rolling pin
2 Paintbrushes
Corn syrup
Dress cookie
Pastry bag with #2 tip
White royal icing
Tulle
Knife or border cutter
Super Pearl Luster Dust
Ribbons

*Remember: You can always add layers to any cookie you make. Just remember to roll the layers thinner than the base layer.*

## DIRECTIONS:

Roll fondant on parchment paper until it is ⅛-inch thick. Cut it with the cookie cutter then cut off the top of the gown and save for later use. Roll over the skirt once with a textured rolling pin. Use a paintbrush to dab corn syrup on the skirt part of your cookie. Carefully place the fondant on the cookie, smoothing the edges with a dry finger.

Pipe white royal icing onto the waist part of the cookie (on top of the fondant) and attach the tulle. The tulle can cover the entire cookie or only part of it—whatever you prefer.

Roll more white fondant, thinner than the base fondant. Cut with the cookie cutter, then cut away the bust area with a knife or border cutter. Dab corn syrup onto the bust area of your cookie, and on top of the tulle, and add this thin layer of fondant. This will create layers, like a bustier.

With the unused paintbrush, brush pearl dust on the dress.

Pipe royal icing detail and use to attach ribbons.

Let dry for at least one hour or until the fondant is hardened.

*Another idea:* For a less decorative dress, simply use the base layer of fondant and adhere ribbons to the cookie with royal icing. No tulle or fondant layers necessary.

● **Abbey says:** My mom believes that when it comes to cookie decorating, you can never use too much "stuff"—our couture line is proof.

# BABY MINE

# Carriage

*The baby favor collection is one of our most popular collections.*

---

**Mix and match pastel colors for a baby shower or spark conversation with several cookie designs.**

## WHAT YOU NEED:

Parchment paper
Colored fondant
Fondant rolling pin
Carriage cookie cutter
Paintbrush
Corn syrup
Carriage cookie
White royal icing
Pastry bag with #2 tip
Sugar flowers
Ribbons

## DIRECTIONS:

Roll fondant on parchment paper until it is ⅛-inch thick. Cut the fondant with the carriage cookie cutter. Paint the top of a cookie with corn syrup. Carefully place the fondant on top of the cookie and smooth the edges with a dry finger.

Pipe royal icing outline and details on your carriage. Work in sections, first the top and then the middle and then the wheels. Pipe a dot onto the center of the wheels and adhere sugar flowers.

Tie a bow and adhere it to the top middle part of the carriage.

Let dry for at least one hour or until the fondant is hardened.

*Another idea:* When we want a really full bow, we tie two ribbons together.

● **Margie says:** I love these cookies! They remind me of the fussy carriages seen in many antiques stores.

# Bibs

*Our baby-themed cookies are some of our most popular.*
*They naturally make wonderful shower favors, but are always*
*a welcome gift for those awaiting a new addition to their family.*

**WHAT YOU NEED:**

Parchment paper
Fondant—2 colors
Fondant rolling pin
Bib cookie cutter
Paintbrush
Corn syrup
Bib cookie
Textured fondant rolling pin
Knife
White royal icing
Pastry bag with #2 tip
Sugar flower
Ribbons

**DIRECTIONS:**

Roll fondant on parchment paper until it is ⅛-inch thick. Cut fondant with the bib cookie cutter. Paint the top of a cookie with corn syrup. Carefully place the fondant on top of the cookie and smooth the edges with a dry finger.

Roll your accent fondant on parchment to ⅛-inch thick. Roll textured rolling pin once over the fondant. Cut with cookie cutter and trim to create a smaller bib shape. Dab corn syrup on top section of the base fondant and layer bib cut out on top.

Pipe royal icing accents and use it to adhere the sugar flower and ribbons. Let dry for at least one hour or until the fondant is hardened.

# Rattle

*Celebrate a sweet arrival with sweet cookies.*

———◆•◆•◆———

Parchment paper
Colored fondant
Fondant rolling pin
Rattle cookie cutter
Paintbrush
Corn syrup
Rattle cookie
White royal icing
Pastry bag with #2 tip
Ribbons

**DIRECTIONS:**

Roll fondant on parchment paper until it is ⅛-inch thick. Cut with a rattle-shaped cookie cutter. Paint the top of a cookie with corn syrup. Carefully place the fondant on top of the cookie and smooth the edges with a dry finger.

Use white royal icing to pipe detail on your rattle and to adhere ribbons to your cookie.

Let dry for at least one hour or until the fondant is hardened.

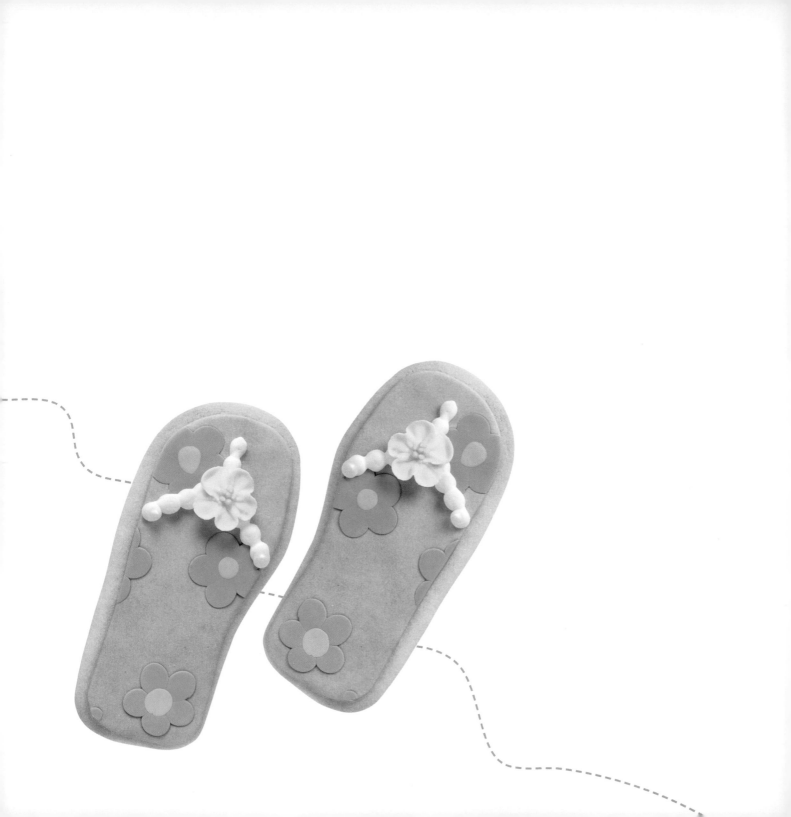

# AT THE BEACH

# Beach Umbrella

*Somewhere on the French Riviera, these beach umbrellas shade beach goers. With colors that mimic the colors of the sea, these cookies are sure to evoke the sights and sounds of summer!*

---

**WHAT YOU NEED:**

Colored fondant
White fondant
Parchment paper
Fondant rolling pin
Umbrella cookie cutter
2 Paintbrushes
Corn syrup
Umbrella cookie on a stick
Pastry bag with #2 tip
White royal icing
Ribbons
Gold Pearl Luster Dust

**DIRECTIONS:**

Mix colored and white fondant until you get a swirled effect.

Roll fondant on parchment paper until it is ⅛-inch thick. Use your cookie cutter to cut the fondant. Paint the cookie with corn syrup. Carefully place the fondant on the cookie and smooth the edges with a dry finger.

Use white royal icing and pipe details of umbrella. Be playful with the designs of the royal icing.

Adhere ribbon to top of umbrella with royal icing.

With unused paintbrush, paint Gold Pearl Dust on umbrella.

Let dry for at least one hour or until the fondant is hardened.

*Another idea:* Going to a shower rather than the beach? Simply bake the cookie with the stem instead of the stick and use pastel fondant for a bridal shower favor.

---

**Remember:** *You can use your cookie cutters for a variety of shapes, as long as you're creative! For these cookies, we used an umbrella cookie cutter, cut off the dough handle and replaced it with a lollypop stick. But remember to cut the umbrella handle off before you bake the cookie!*

# Bare Feet

*Abbey says: My mom loves playing with my nieces at the beach. This design was inspired by the idea of sand stuck all over their little toes!*

———◆———

**WHAT YOU NEED:**

Parchment paper
White fondant
Fondant rolling pin
Feet cookie cutter
Paintbrush
Corn syrup
Feet cookie
Pastry bag with #2 tip
Pink or red royal icing
Natural (Raw) sugar crystals

**DIRECTIONS:**

Roll fondant on parchment paper until it is ⅛-inch thick. Use your cookie cutter to cut the fondant. Paint the cookie with corn syrup. Carefully place the fondant on the cookie and smooth the edges with a dry finger.

Pipe royal icing on the toes as nail polish.

Lightly paint corn syrup on top of the fondant and sprinkle with sugar crystals. Shake off excess.

Let dry for at least one hour or until the fondant is hardened.

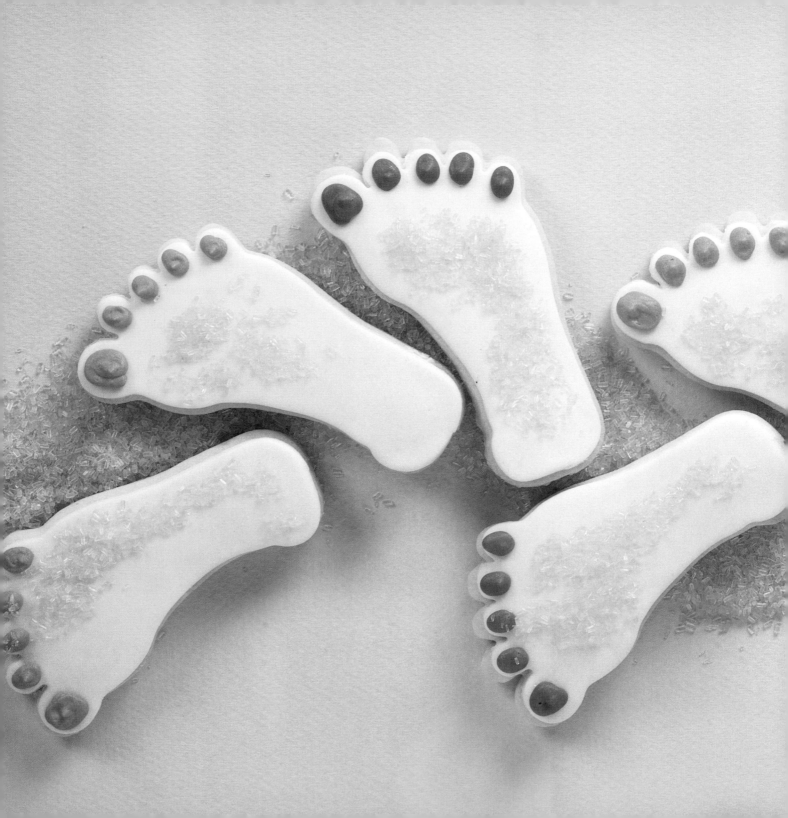

# Fish

*These cookies are so much fun!*
*We just love how the fish look, swimming among the bubbles.*

———◆———

These fish require just a bit of assembling but most of the accessories can be made a day in advance.

**WHAT YOU NEED:**

Parchment paper
Fondant–2 colors
Fondant rolling pin
Fish cookie cutter
Paintbrush
Corn syrup
Fish cookie
Small circle cookie cutters
Pastry bag with #2 tip
White royal icing
Black royal icing

**DIRECTIONS:**

Roll fondant on parchment paper until it is ⅛-inch thick. Cut with your fish cookie cutter. Paint the top of a cookie with corn syrup. Carefully place the fondant on top of the cookie and smooth the edges with a dry finger.

Roll accent fondants to ⅛-inch thick. Using your small circular cutters, cut out circles in various sizes. Set aside.

Dab corn syrup on the back of your fondant circles, or bubbles, and carefully arrange them on your fish.

Pipe white royal icing accents onto your fish's fins. Pipe a dot for his eye and finish it off by piping a black dot on top of the white.

Let dry for at least one hour or until the fondant is hardened.

*Remember: Layering your fondant accents creates a multi-dimensional design. Try it here with the bubble accents.*

# Buxom Bikini

*This cookie always gets a reaction!*

———◆———

**Use a variety of candies for a variety of cup sizes!**

## WHAT YOU NEED:

Fondant rolling pin
Fondant—2 colors
Parchment paper
Bikini cookie cutter
Paintbrush
Corn syrup
Round candies
Bikini cookie
Pastry bag with #2 tip
White royal icing
Ribbons or sugar flowers

## DIRECTIONS:

Roll the fondant on parchment paper until it is ⅛-inch thick. To make an itsy bitsy polka dot bikini, roll small balls of accent color and place on rolled fondant. Roll until flat. Cut out the top and bottom of the bikini with your cookie cutters.

Paint corn syrup on the top of your cookie. Place 2 candies on the brassiere part of the bikini top cookie. Carefully place fondant on top of the cookie and candies and smooth the edges with a dry finger. Adhere fondant bottom onto cookie bottom.

Pipe white royal icing detail and use the icing to adhere a bow or sugar flower.

Let dry for at least one hour or until the fondant is hardened.

● **Margie says:** We are always looking for ways to add dimension and texture to our cookies, and we often do this with accessories such as candies or ribbons. While playing around with a bathing suit design, Karen, the Flour Pot "fondant Queen," cleverly put some accessories under the fondant rather that over it. We were hysterical in the kitchen.

● **Abbey says:** When I walked into the kitchen to see what was going on, I found bikinis with 3-dimensional tops.

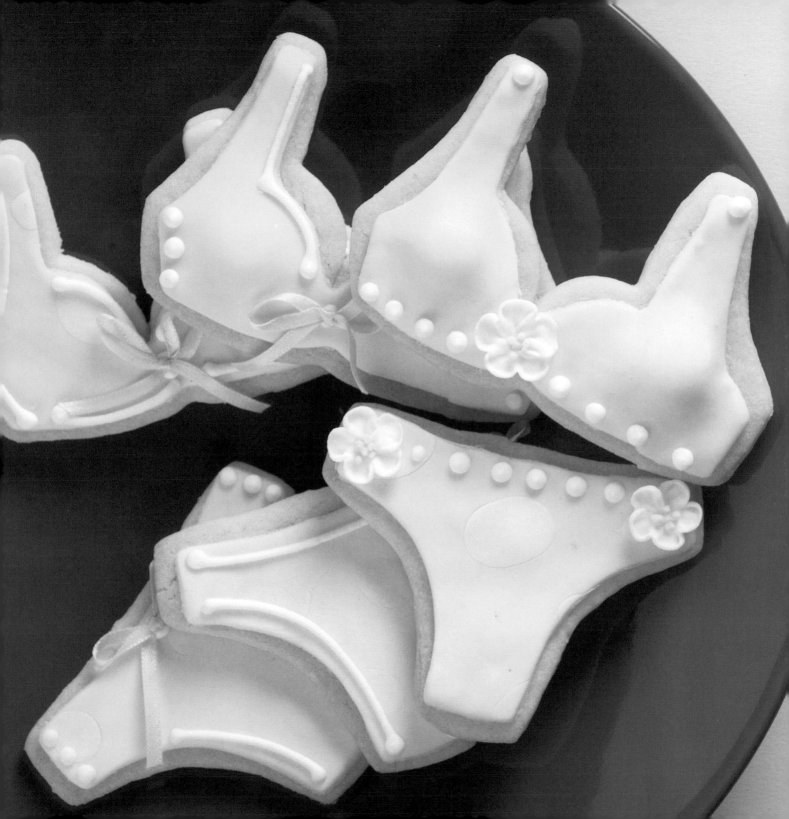

# Flip Flops

*Flip flops are such a big fashion accessory, and not just at the beach!*

———◆———

Add these cookies to the menu for your next beach house party and your very fashionable guests will be delightfully surprised!

**WHAT YOU NEED:**

Parchment paper
Fondant—2 colors
Fondant rolling pin
Small cookie cutters in any shape
Small flower cookie cutters
Shoe cookie cutter
Paintbrush
Corn syrup
Shoe cookie
White royal icing
Pastry bag with #2 tip
Sugar flowers

**DIRECTIONS:**

Roll base fondant on parchment paper until it is ⅛-inch thick. Set aside.

Roll accent fondant until it is ⅛-inch thick. Use small cutters to cut out shapes from your accent fondant. Place these shapes on base fondant and roll until flat.

Cut flip flop shape with your cookie cutter. Paint the top of a cookie with corn syrup. Carefully place the fondant on top of the cookie and smooth the edges with a dry finger.

Starting at the top and moving down the right side, pipe a strap on your flip flop with royal icing. Then pipe the left side of the strap. It's similar to a sideways "Y". Adhere a sugar flower in the center of the strap.

Let dry for at least one hour or until the fondant is hardened.

*Another idea:* Polka dots or stripe patterns also work nicely here, especially if you don't have small cookie cutters to cut out designs.

**Remember:** *Small fondant designs will change shape when you roll them out, so try not to choose cutters that have a lot of detail. The new designs are always a surprise, but always one of a kind.*

*Use any tip or technique for the strap, or play around with different colors of icing.*

# Sail Boat

*These sail boats remind us of trips to the Chesapeake Bay
and the boats out in the harbor.*

---

**Be creative with the color of your sails or stick with the nautical theme of blue and white.**

## WHAT YOU NEED:

Parchment paper
White fondant
Fondant rolling pin
Red fondant
Sail boat cookie cutter
Paintbrush
Corn syrup
Sail boat cookie
Colored fondant
Small triangular cookie cutter or knife
Lollipop stick
Pastry bag with #2 tip
White royal icing
Blue royal icing

## DIRECTIONS:

Roll base fondant on parchment paper until it is ⅛-inch thick. Set aside.

Create thin ropes of red fondant and place on top of white fondant. Roll until ⅛-inch thick.

Use your cookie cutter to cut the fondant, making sure the red stripes are included in the sail. Take your paintbrush and paint the top of a cookie with corn syrup. Carefully place the fondant on top of the cookie and smooth the edges with a dry finger.

Roll the accent fondant until it's ⅛-inch thick. Cut out triangle shapes and lay them on top of the lollipop stick to create a bend in the triangle (this will make the triangles look like a sail blowing in the wind). Repeat for each color flag. Let dry for 15 minutes or until hard.

Pipe royal icing on your lollipop stick and adhere it to the middle of the cookie. Attach flags with royal icing.

Pipe blue icing for the ocean water.

Let dry for at least one hour or until the fondant is hardened.

---

***Remember:*** *Fondant dries out quickly, so work fast. For this cookie, make all of your flags at one time. They will harden in a 3-dimensional shape. You can make these flags ahead of time.*

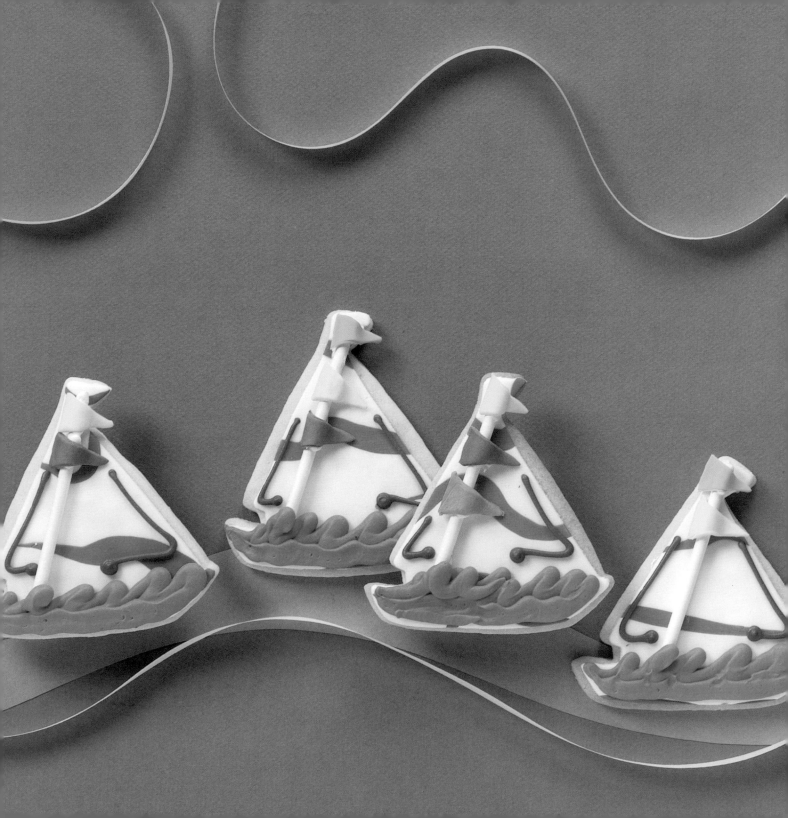

TRICK OR TREAT!

# Witch's Hat

*While many images of witches can be scary, we imagine
the witch who owns this hat to be sexy and swift!*

## WHAT YOU NEED:

Fondant rolling pin
Black fondant
Parchment paper
Hat cookie cutter
Bat cookie cutter
Paintbrush
Corn syrup
Hat cookie
Pastry bag with #2 tip
Black royal icing
Yellow royal icing
Ribbons

## DIRECTIONS:

Roll fondant on parchment paper until it is ⅛-inch thick. Cut it with your hat cookie cutter.

Cut out a bat shape with the bat cookie cutter. Gently bend the bat's wings so it looks like it is flying. Set the bat aside.

Use a paintbrush to dab corn syrup on the top of your hat cookie. Carefully place fondant on the cookie, smoothing the edges with a dry finger. Create a ruffle in the brim of your hat by shaping the fondant in your hands.

Pipe detail on hat with black royal icing.

Take a piece of ribbon and fold it in a "V" shape. Use icing to adhere the center of the "V" to the part of your hat where the brim meets the cap. This will make it look like the ribbon is being whipped in the wind as the witch flies on her broom!

Pipe yellow royal icing eyes on the bat and let dry. Adhere the bat on top of the ribbon where it is attached to the hat.

Let dry for at least one hour or until the fondant is hardened.

---

**Remember:** *Colored icing can stain your hands, so use gloves when mixing fondant colors or when working with deeply colored fondants. Beware of black icing—you, too, may end up looking spooky!*

*When ruffling the brim of the hat, don't put corn syrup on the part that forms the ruffle. You don't want it to stick to the cookie.*

---

# Jack-O-Lantern

*We can just hear the bats fluttering around on Halloween night!*

<hr/>

**WHAT YOU NEED:**

Fondant rolling pin
Orange fondant
Parchment paper
Small bat cookie cutter
Black fondant
Leaf stamp
Pumpkin cookie cutter
2 Paintbrushes
Corn syrup
Cookie
Gold Pearl Luster Dust
Scoring tool or toothpick
Pastry bag with #2 tip
Black royal icing

**DIRECTIONS:**

Roll the orange fondant on parchment paper until it is ⅛-inch thick. Cut out three bats.

Roll black fondant until it is ⅛-inch thick. Cut out three bats. With a leaf stamp, cut out a black leaf. Set aside.

Place the black bat cut outs into the bat-shaped holes left in the orange fondant. Roll the fondant roller once over this to join all pieces of fondant.

Cut with the pumpkin cookie cutter. Use a paintbrush to dab corn syrup on the top of your pumpkin cookie. Carefully place fondant on the cookie, smoothing the edges with a dry finger.

With unused paintbrush, dust cookie with gold pearl dust.

Use scoring tool or toothpick to create the lines on the outside of the pumpkin.

Pipe a stem and vine with black icing. Adhere the leaf to the royal icing.

Let dry for at least one hour or until the fondant is hardened.

*Another idea:* Use same technique and cut out different designs. Spell BOO with letters or use small cutter shapes to make a spooky face.

# Candy Corn

*Abbey says: When I was away at college, my mom used to send me these cookies in place of real candy corn for Halloween treats.*

———◆———

These cookies are made all the more festive when wrapped in cellophane and tied with raffia bows.

## WHAT YOU NEED:

Parchment paper
Fondant rolling pin
Yellow fondant
Orange fondant
White fondant
Knife
Triangle cookie cutter
Paintbrush
Corn syrup
Triangle cookie

## DIRECTIONS:

Roll yellow fondant on parchment paper until it is ⅛-inch thick. Cut fondant into ½-inch thick strips. Set aside. Repeat these steps with the white and orange fondants.

Place the strips of fondant side-by-side on the parchment. Roll until the strips become one piece of fondant.

Cut out a candy corn shape with your cookie cutter. Use a paintbrush to dab corn syrup on the top of your cookie. Carefully place fondant on the cookie, smoothing the edges with a dry finger.

Let dry for at least one hour or until the fondant is hardened.

*Another idea:* Sometimes a fairly simple cookie can be turned into a wonderful conversation piece due to the packaging alone.

# Lollies and Suckers

*These cookies look like the giant old-fashioned lollies your mom would never let you buy! Just imagine all the fun colors you can use!*

---

## WHAT YOU NEED:

Colored fondant

Parchment paper

Fondant rolling pin

Circle cookie cutter

Paint brush

Corn syrup

Circle cookies on a stick

Ribbons and cellophane (optional)

---

**Remember:** *Work fast with your fondant. Don't let it sit too long or it will dry out.*

---

## DIRECTIONS:

With your hands, create thin ropes of fondant, approximately ½-inch in diameter. For a 3-inch cookie, you need the rope to be 15 inches long. Repeat this process with different colors of fondant.

Place the fondant ropes next to each other on the parchment. Coil this rope so it forms a circle. As you twist, keep the coil flat on the parchment and press down lightly on the center. Be careful not to smash the center.

Roll the coil out, starting at the center and rolling lightly in all directions until the individual ropes are integrated into each other and the fondant is ⅛-inch thick.

Cut out a circle with your cookie cutter. Look at both sides of the circle to decide which side looks best. Paint corn syrup on a cookie and carefully place the fondant circle on the cookie, with the best looking side up. Smooth the sides with your fingers. Cover one cookie at a time.

Let dry for at least one hour or until the fondant is hardened.

Tie ribbons around the stick at the base of each cookie or wrap each cookie in cellophane and tie the ends with ribbons.

For the suckers, follow the instructions above but use a cookie without a stick. Wrap the sucker in cellophane and tie the ends with ribbons.

*Another idea:* It's fun to experiment with different amounts and thickness of fondant ropes for different looks.

Create themed centerpieces: Place your cookies in popcorn boxes for a carnival theme or stick them out of a Styrofoam ball for a Candy Land theme.

# SEASONAL DELIGHTS

# Fall Leaves

*We can just feel the crispness of the fall air when we look at these cookies.*
*The super pearl dust makes your leaves glisten like they are kissed with morning dew.*

---

**These cookies are great if you're learning to work with fondant. They are also devoid of piping.**
**Don't worry about wasting fondant with these cookies, it's ok if it all ends up brown!**

## WHAT YOU NEED:

3 fall-colored fondants
Parchment paper
Fondant rolling pin
Leaf cookie cutter
2 Paintbrushes
Corn syrup
Leaf cookie
Toothpick
Super Pearl Luster Dust

## DIRECTIONS:

Using your hands, combine the fondants until they you get a swirled effect. Do not mix too much or your color will be murky.

Roll fondant on parchment paper until it is ⅛-inch thick. Cut with the leaf cookie cutter. Paint the top of a cookie with corn syrup. Carefully place the fondant on top of the cookie and smooth the edges with a dry finger.

While the fondant is still soft, use a toothpick to vein the leaves. Press firmly but work in a fluid motion. Immediately dust the cookie with Super Pearl Dust with your remaining paintbrush for a sparkly finish.

Let dry for at least one hour or until the fondant is hardened.

*Another idea:* Make green leaves as accents for spring-themed cookies!

---

*Remember: When you decorate and accent your fondant, don't worry about it being perfect. Don't think too much about creating the leaf's veins or where they should go, just let your hand do the work. With practice and a relaxed outlook, you'll become a natural!*

---

● **Abbey says:** My favorite season is fall, so this is one of my favorite cookies.
● **Margie says:** Although they look difficult, these cookies couldn't be simpler as long as you have the right tools. I like to use a special tool I call my "lethal weapon"—a glorified toothpick!

# Snowflakes

*The icy blues and purples make these snowflakes look cool.*

**WHAT YOU NEED:**

Blue fondant
White fondant
Parchment paper
Fondant rolling pin
Snowflake cookie cutter
2 Paintbrushes
Corn syrup
Snowflake cookie
Super Pearl Luster Dust
Pastry bag with #2 tip
White royal icing

**DIRECTIONS:**

Using your hands, combine the blue and white fondants until you get a swirled look. Roll the fondant on parchment paper until it is ⅛-inch thick. Cut it with your cookie cutter.

Paint corn syrup on the top of your cookie. Carefully place fondant on the cookie, smoothing the edges with a dry finger.

With the unused paintbrush, dust the cookie with Super Pearl Dust.

Pipe detail with white royal icing.

Let dry for at least one hour or until the fondant is hardened.

*Another idea:* For extra sparkle, add a dragée to the center of your snowflake. Or make your cookie an edible ornament for friends and family. Before baking, poke a hole in your cookie. After you decorate, string a ribbon through the hole.

# Mittens

*You don't want to lose these mittens!*

———————————◆———————————

**WHAT YOU NEED:**

Parchment paper
Fondant rolling pin
Colored fondant
Knife
White fondant
Mitten cookie cutter
Paintbrush
Corn syrup
Mitten cookie
Border cutter
Pastry bag with #2 tip
White royal icing
Sugar flowers
Ribbons

**DIRECTIONS:**

Roll colored fondant on parchment paper until it is ⅛-inch thick. Cut at least five strips of ½-inch wide fondant. Set aside. Repeat with white fondant.

Lay the strips side by side, alternating the colors. Carefully roll until the strips become one piece of fondant. Cut with your mitten cookie cutter. Paint corn syrup on the top of your cookie. Carefully place fondant on the cookie, smoothing the edges with a dry finger.

Place balls of white fondant on top of leftover rolled colored fondant. Roll more if necessary. Roll the balls into the fondant and use the border cutter to cut a ½-inch wide trim for your mittens. Adhere to the bottom of your mitten with royal icing.

Outline the cookie with royal icing and pipe on some dot embellishments. Adhere flowers and ribbon with royal icing.

Let dry for at least one hour or until the fondant is hardened.

*Another idea:* For a less complicated trim, simply adhere sugar flowers to the bottom of the mitten.

# Santa

*This Santa is straight from the North Pole, rosy cheeks and all!*
*Can't you just imagine his full belly?!*

————◆————

Many people, novices and experts alike, bake Christmas cookies.
Decorating them is a great way to include kids in the holiday festivities.

## WHAT YOU NEED:

Fondant rolling pin
Red fondant
Parchment paper
Santa with a hat cookie cutter
Knife
3 Paintbrushes
Corn syrup
Santa cookie
White fondant
Pastry bag with # 18 star tip
White royal icing
Sprinkles
#2 tip
Red royal icing
Black royal icing
Super Red Luster Dust
Super Pearl Luster Dust

## DIRECTIONS:

Roll red fondant on parchment paper until it is ⅛-inch thick. Cut the fondant with your cookie cutter. Use the knife to separate the hat from the rest of the Santa. We cut on the diagonal, as opposed to straight across, so Santa's hat is tilted on his head.

Paint corn syrup on the cookie where Santa's hat will go. Carefully place the fondant hat on the cookie, smoothing the edges with a dry finger.

Roll out the white fondant. Cut with the Santa cookie cutter and cut out the beard. Adhere the fondant to the cookie.

With a #18 tip on your piping bag, pipe white royal icing stars as trim on the hat. Pipe one star on the tip of the hat like a pom pom. Drizzle some sprinkles on the pom pom.

Use your #2 tip and pipe a royal icing moustache.

Pipe a red dot, or nose, in the center of Santa's moustache.

Pipe 2 black icing dots for the eyes.

With an unused paintbrush, dust Red Luster Dust on the hat and cheeks.

Use the third paintbrush to dust the moustache with Super Pearl Dust.

Let dry for at least one hour or until the fondant is hardened.

———————————————

***Remember:*** *When the directions call for a knife to trim the fondant, be creative. If you're not confident cutting a straight line, you can always use the edges of other cookie cutters.*

# Ice Skate

*The attention to detail makes these ice skates really special.*

---

**WHAT YOU NEED:**

Parchment paper
Fondant rolling pin
Colored fondant
Ice Skate cookie cutter
#2 tip
Toothpick
2 Paintbrushes
Corn syrup
Ice Skate cookie
Tracing wheel (found in sewing stores)
Pasty bag
White royal icing
Nu Silver Luster Dust Paint
(see recipe below)

**DIRECTIONS:**

Roll fondant on parchment paper until it is ⅛-inch thick. Cut it with your cookie cutter.

Use the end of a #2 pastry tip and cut out small circles for the shoelaces. Clean out the tip with a toothpick.

Paint corn syrup on the top of your cookie. Carefully place fondant on the cookie, smoothing the edges with a dry finger.

While fondant is soft, use a tracing wheel to create stitch effect on skate. Try not to stop and start in the middle of a line.

With an unused paintbrush, paint the blade of the skate with Nu Silver Luster Dust Paint. Go over it until it is not streaky.

Pipe royal icing laces and skate detail.

Let dry for at least one hour or until the fondant is hardened.

**NU SILVER LUSTER DUST PAINT**

½ teaspoon Nu Silver Luster Dust
One drop lemon extract

**DIRECTIONS:**

Mix Nu Silver Dust with lemon extract in a small dish. Mix with paintbrush to create pasty consistency.

# Ice Cream Cones

*What could be better than a drip-free ice cream cone in the summertime?!*

---

**These cookies are also great for kid's birthdays.**

**WHAT YOU NEED:**

Fondant—2 colors
Fondant rolling pin
Parchment paper
Ice Cream cookie cutter
Knife
Paintbrush
Corn syrup
Ice Cream cookie
Pastry bag with #2 tip
White royal icing
Red royal icing
Brown royal icing

**DIRECTIONS:**

Combine fondants with your hands until you get a swirled look.

Roll fondant on parchment paper until it is ⅛-inch thick. Cut it with your cookie cutter. With a knife, separate the ice cream from the cone. Remember to trim it so it looks like an ice cream scoop (in other words do not trim straight).

Paint corn syrup on the top of your cookie. Carefully place fondant on the cookie, smoothing the edges with a dry finger.

Pipe white royal icing detail on the ice cream.

Pipe red royal icing to create a cherry on top of the fondant.

Pipe a grid pattern on the cone with brown royal icing.

Let dry for at least one hour or until the fondant is hardened.

*Another idea:* Sometimes a great cookie shape comes from just thinking outside the box. This ice cream cone may look simple, but turn it upside down and it is our more complicated friend, the clown!

Seek out new uses for your favorite cutters. It not only allows you to create a custom shapes, but it is more economical.

# Sun

*Did you know that the heat in the center of the sun is 25,000,000 degrees?!*
*That's what we think of when we roll the bright orange and yellow fondants.*
*These colors and swirls make you feel warm.*

━━━◆━━━

Add an unconventional cookie prop, like kids' sunglasses, and you have a fun in the sun cookie design.

**WHAT YOU NEED:**

Orange fondant

Yellow fondant

Parchment paper

Fondant rolling pin

Sun cookie cutter

2 Paintbrushes

Corn syrup

Sun cookie

Gold Pearl Luster Dust

Pastry bag with #2 tip

Yellow royal icing

Small sunglasses without the arms

Sugar flowers

**DIRECTIONS:**

With your hands, combine the orange and yellow fondants until you get a swirled look. Roll on parchment paper until it is ⅛-inch thick. Cut it with your cookie cutter.

Paint corn syrup on the top of your cookie. Carefully place fondant on the cookie, smoothing the edges with a dry finger.

With the unused paintbrush, dust the fondant with Gold Pearl Dust.

Pipe an outline of the sun and a mouth with yellow royal icing. Adhere sunglasses to cookie with royal icing. Adhere sugar flowers to the sunglasses.

Let dry for at least one hour or until the fondant is hardened.

*Another idea:* Instead of using sunglasses, draw a face on your sun cookie with royal icing.

CELEBRATE SPRING

# Easter Egg Basket

*Every Easter, little children hunt for Easter eggs in Rittenhouse Square in Philadelphia. We love watching the kids in their pastel dresses and child-size ties, giggling and running around. We imagine that if they carried baskets, those baskets would look like these.*

The decorations on this cookie always surprise people, especially when we tell them how we do it. The basket weave is simply created with a basket weave patterned rolling pin. Just one roll over the fondant and you're done!

**WHAT YOU NEED:**

Parchment paper
Fondant rolling pin
Colored fondant
Textured fondant rolling pin (basket weave)
Oval cookie cutter
Knife
Paintbrush
Corn syrup
Oval cookie
Pastry bag with #2 tip
White royal icing
Green royal icing
Egg shaped candies
Ribbons

**DIRECTIONS:**

Roll fondant on parchment paper until it is ⅛-inch thick. Roll once over the fondant with the basket weave rolling pin. Cut it with your cookie cutter. Trim the oval in half with a knife.

Paint corn syrup on the bottom half of your cookie. Carefully place fondant on the bottom part of the cookie, smoothing the edges with a dry finger.

Create two thin ropes of fondant. Twist together into one rope for the handle. Adhere with white royal icing to the top of your cookie. Trim excess with the knife.

On the top of your basket, so it looks like it's coming out of the basket, pipe green royal icing grass.

Adhere egg-shaped candies on top of the grass. Add more icing under the candy if necessary to secure candies.

Tie ribbons and add bows to the side of the basket with more green royal icing.

Accent the basket with dots of white royal icing.

Let dry for at least one hour or until the fondant is hardened.

# Fashionista Chick

*Add this cookie to your Easter basket for an extra special treat.*

---

## WHAT YOU NEED:

Parchment paper
Yellow fondant
Fondant rolling pin
Chick cookie cutter
Paintbrush
Corn syrup
Chick cookie
White fondant
Small heart cookie cutter
Pink fondant
Textured fondant rolling pin
Knife
Super Pearl Luster Dust
Pastry bag with #2 tip
White royal icing
Sugar flowers
Sugar leaves
Orange royal icing
Black royal icing
Ribbons (optional)

## DIRECTIONS:

Roll yellow fondant on parchment paper until it is ⅛-inch thick. Cut with your chick cookie cutter. Paint the top of a cookie with corn syrup. Carefully place the fondant on top of the cookie and smooth the edges with a dry finger.

Roll the white fondant to ⅛-inch thickness and cut out a heart with your small cookie cutter. This will be the chick's wing. Dab a bit of corn syrup where the chick's wing should go and carefully adhere the heart so that the point of the heart is pointing toward the chick's beak. Repeat with yellow fondant, laying the two heart-shaped wings.

Roll pink fondant to ⅛-inch thickness and roll it once with the textured rolling pin. Use a knife to cut out a small cap for the chick. Adhere this to the chick's head with corn syrup.

While fondant is still soft, dust Super Pearl Dust on the entire cookie.

Pipe royal icing dots onto a corner of the hat and adhere leaves and flower adornments or a bow. You can also add these to the area around the chick's feet so it looks like he's walking in a garden. Pipe a white eye for the chick and accent dots on the wing.

Pipe an orange royal icing beak.

Pipe a black royal icing dot in the chick's white eye.

Let dry for at least one hour or until the fondant is hardened.

---

***Remember:*** *Textured rolling pins are always optional, but they sure give your cookies a nice look!*

---

# Polka Dot Eggs

*Add a new tradition to your Easter celebration
with this modern twist on egg decorating.*

---

**WHAT YOU NEED:**

Parchment paper
Fondant rolling pin
Fondant—2 colors
Oval cookie cutter
Paintbrush
Corn syrup
Oval cookie

**DIRECTIONS:**

Roll base fondant on parchment paper until it is ⅛-inch thick. Create small pea-sized balls with accent fondant and place randomly on the base color. Roll until flat. Cut it with your cookie cutter.

Paint corn syrup on the top of your cookie. Carefully place fondant on the cookie, smoothing the edges with a dry finger.

Let dry for at least one hour or until the fondant is hardened.

# Tulips

*What flower evokes spring better than a tulip?*

Fondant—2 colors
Parchment paper
Fondant rolling pin
Tulip cookie cutter
Paintbrush
Corn syrup
Tulip cookie on a stick
Knife
Paper towels
Pastry bag with #2 tip
White royal icing
Floral tape
Silk leaf

**DIRECTIONS:**

Combine both fondants in your hands until you get a swirled effect. Roll fondant on parchment paper until it is ⅛-inch thick. You want the fondant to have striations that resemble the markings of a parrot tulip. Cut it with your cookie cutter.

Paint corn syrup on the top of your cookie. Carefully place fondant on the cookie, smoothing the edges with a dry finger.

Cut another tulip out of your fondant. Roll it so it is a little thinner than the first. Cut the tulip in half to create two petals.

Dab corn syrup on the base of your fondant cookie and carefully adhere a petal. Ruffle the edge of the petal and hold in place with crushed paper towels. Repeat with the other petal.

Pipe white royal icing accents on the fondant.

Let dry for at least one hour or until the fondant is hardened.

Starting at the top, wrap the cookie stick with floral tape. Attach the leaf with floral tape.

*Another idea:* Solid colored fondant looks very pretty on these cookies. Consider arranging your finished cookies in a terra cotta pot for a party centerpiece or a basket for a holiday celebration.

**Remember:** *None of your cookies must adhere to the rules of nature. None of your colors, details, or decorations have to be true to life.*

# ROCKIN'
# FOURTH OF JULY!

# Stars

*These cookies are simple to make and great for
a Fourth of July dessert buffet or picnic.*

## WHAT YOU NEED:

Colored fondant

Parchment paper

Fondant rolling pin

Star cookie cutter

2 Paintbrushes

Corn syrup

Star cookie

Super Pearl Luster Dust

## DIRECTIONS:

Roll fondant on parchment paper until it is ⅛-inch thick. Cut it with your cookie cutter. Use a paintbrush to dab corn syrup on the top of your cookie. Carefully place fondant on the cookie, smoothing the edges with a dry finger.

Use unused paintbrush to brush cookie with Super Pearl Dust.

Let dry for at least one hour or until the fondant is hardened.

● **Abbey says:** My dad's birthday is June 14th—Flag Day—so naturally, my mom always has a flag day themed party for him.

● **Margie says:** I spend all year gathering red, white, and blue items. And every year, I make these cookies.

# Liberty Bell

*From the City of Brotherly Love, our Liberty Bell cookies are great souvenirs and are even better for reminding us that 4th of July celebrations are about independence!*

---

## WHAT YOU NEED:

Fondant rolling pin
Colored fondant
Parchment paper
Bell cookie cutter
Paintbrush
Corn syrup
Bell cookie
Pastry bag with #2 tip
Red royal icing
White royal icing
Blue royal icing
Dragées

## DIRECTIONS:

Roll the fondant on parchment paper until it is ⅛-inch thick. Cut it with your cookie cutter.

Paint corn syrup on the top of your cookie. Carefully place fondant on the cookie, smoothing the edges with a dry finger.

Pipe a royal icing outline of the bell and it's famous crack. Carefully adhere dragées to the piping on the bottom of the bell.

Let dry for at least one hour or until the fondant is hardened.

# Guitar

*This guitar is just as sweet as its imaginary sounds!*

**WHAT YOU NEED:**

Parchment paper
Fondant rolling pin
Chocolate fondant
Guitar cookie cutter
2 Paintbrushes
Corn syrup
Guitar cookie
Colored fondant
Small circular cutter
Pastry bag with #2 tip
White royal icing
Thin ribbons
Dragées
Candies

**DIRECTIONS:**

Roll chocolate fondant on parchment paper until it is ⅛-inch thick. Cut it with your cookie cutter. Use a paintbrush to dab corn syrup on the top of your cookie. Carefully place fondant on the cookie, smoothing the edges with a dry finger.

Roll accent fondant until it is ⅛-inch thick. Cut it with a circular cookie cutter and adhere to the guitar.

With white royal icing, adhere thin ribbons as guitar strings from the thin end of the guitar to the end of the accent color circle.

Adhere dragées with royal icing over the ribbon ends and on the thin end of the guitar.

Place a candy on the other end of the strings and adhere with ribbons. Place another candy on the strings on the other side of the accent circle.

Pipe a white royal icing outline of guitar.

Let dry for at least one hour or until the fondant is hardened.

*Another idea:* Play around with candies to decorate your cookies. Candy comes in so many shapes, sizes and colors, you can go wild!

---

*Remember:* Keep your fondant in a sealed plastic bag when you're not using it or it will dry out.

---

● **Margie says:** I think every child growing up in the sixties wanted to learn how to play the guitar. Many notes of "If I Had A Hammer" came out of guitars like this one.

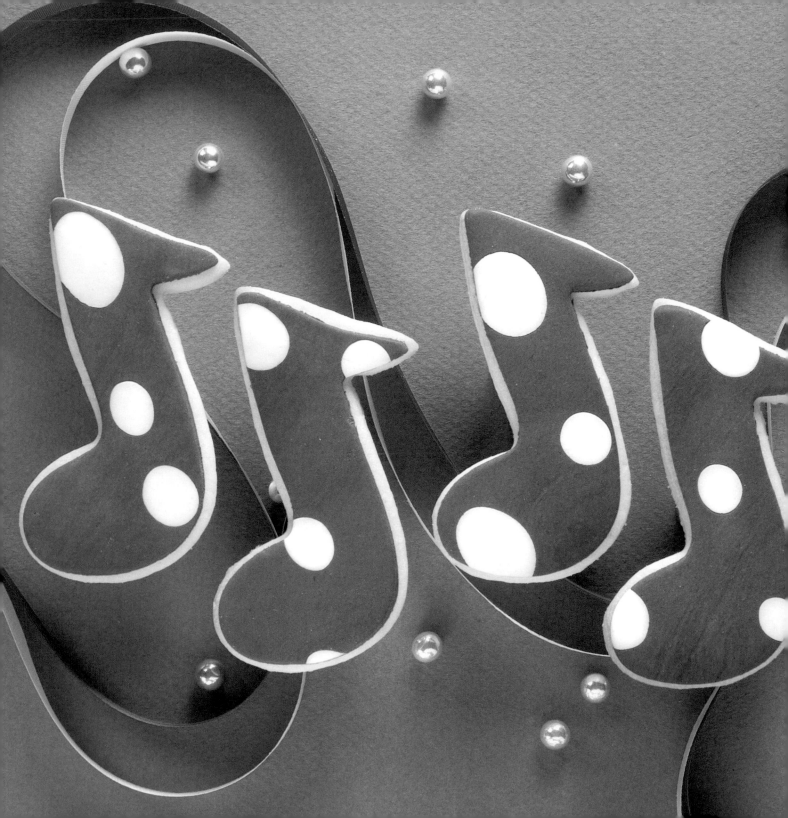

# Music Notes

*Feel the staccato-like tempo as you roll the white dots across this musically inclined fondant. Their elegant but clean design makes them perfect for an evening affair.*

These cookies are great for those who aren't quite comfortable with pastry bag piping. They're also perfect for large parties. Just roll one large slab of base color fondant and cut away. Remember to work quickly!

**WHAT YOU NEED:**

Parchment paper
Fondant rolling pin
Black fondant
White fondant
Music Note cookie cutter
Paintbrush
Corn syrup
Music Note cookie

**DIRECTIONS:**

Roll black fondant on parchment paper until it is ⅛-inch thick. Set aside.

Create small pea-sized balls of white fondant and place randomly on the black fondant. Roll until flat. Use cookie cutter to cut out fondant.

Paint corn syrup on the top of your cookie. Carefully place fondant on the cookie, smoothing the edges with a dry finger.

Let dry for at least one hour or until the fondant is hardened.

*Another idea:* Music notes don't *have* to be black. Jazz them up with any color you like!

*Remember: Use a light touch when you put corn syrup on a small cookie. Make sure it does not leak over the cookie's edge.*

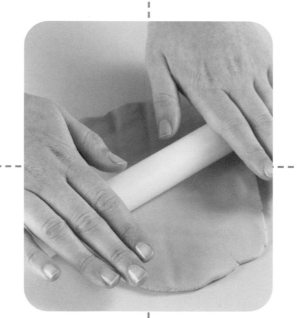

# BASICS

# Cookie Dough

*The first thing people say when they walk into our store is: "It smells so good in here!"*
*There's no smell quite like a kitchen full of fresh baked cookies and this recipe gives*
*you a great base for your cookie masterpieces!*

⸺◆⸺

**Yields approximately 3 dozen (3½-inch) cookies**
**(As Doris, our baker, says, "If you make thinner cookies, you get more, if you like thicker cookies, you get less!")**

**WHAT YOU NEED:**

3 cups (1 pound) all purpose flour
1 teaspoon baking powder
½ pound (2 sticks) unsalted butter,
room temperature
1 cup granulated sugar
1 large egg, room temperature
1 teaspoon pure vanilla extract
Parchment paper

**DIRECTIONS:**

Preheat the oven to 350°F.

In a medium bowl, sift the flour together with the baking powder and set aside. At The Flour Pot, we measure the flour on a scale so it is always exactly the same weight. Sometimes when you scoop it right into the measuring cup, it weighs differently depending upon the way you scoop! If you don't have a kitchen scale, use a spoon to fill a measuring cup with flour and level it off.

In an electric mixing bowl using the paddle attachment, cream together the butter and sugar until light and fluffy. This should take about 3 minutes. Add the egg and vanilla and beat another minute or so.

Add the flour mixture in two batches. Be careful not to add too much at a time or you will be in a snowstorm of flour.

Blend until the dough begins to pull away from the sides of the bowl. Take the dough out of the mixer and place it on a piece of parchment paper. Using your hands, knead the dough for about a minute. Place the dough in a plastic bag and refrigerate for at least an hour. This will make the dough easier to handle when you being to roll it out. However, if you must, you can roll the cookies immediately without refrigeration.

We roll our cookies on parchment paper so there is no need for extra flour. Roll the dough with a rolling pin until it is about ⅛-inch thick. When they bake, these cookies will not really spread, so you can cut the dough out and place them pretty close to each other on a baking tray.

If you are creating a cookie on a stick, this is the time to place lollipop sticks in your cookies.

Bake for 8 minutes or until the cookies begin to take on a golden color. They will continue to cook when removed from the oven, so don't let them get too brown before taking them out.

These cookies also freeze very well. To give them that just baked taste, pop them back in the oven for just a minute or two. But don't freeze the cookies once they are decorated.

# Fondant

Fondant is traditionally used on cakes, but we like to use it on our cookies for an elegant effect. In our classes, we tell people that rolled fondant is like an edible grown up version of clay. It's pliable, can be colored, and dries in whatever shapes and forms you mold it into. Ready-made fondant is available in several sizes, from 1.5-pound packets to 15-pound buckets. We buy white fondant and chocolate flavored fondant. Whenever we need colored fondant, we use gel paste to mix the colors ourselves.

Fondant has a long shelf life. The manufacturers say six months, but we use it so quickly, we've never had to store it that long. However, if you do purchase ready-made fondant, remember that it should not be refrigerated or frozen. We don't freeze decorated cookies either, but I have been told by some loyal customers that if you cover the decorated cookies with plastic wrap and freeze them in an air tight container, the cookies will be ok. Just make sure, when defrosting them, that the condensation is on the plastic wrap and not the cookie.

*Warming fondant in your hands before rolling—it's more pliable.*

Fondant is air sensitive. It is necessary to store fondant in an airtight container or plastic bags with zipper closings. Only take out what you're using or it will begin to dry out.

When using the fondant, warm it up in your hands and roll into a ball shape before rolling it out.

Fondant can be temperamental. It is more difficult to work with in humidity and takes longer to dry. If fondant is too sticky and not rolling properly, add a little bit of corn starch to the fondant.

Fondant is easiest to roll out on parchment paper.

---

***Remember:*** *Your fondant-decorated cookies can take anywhere from a few hours to overnight to dry. Humid weather can affect the drying time as can the thickness of the fondant and the amount of royal icing on the cookie.*

---

## COLORING FONDANT

Remember: Colors are for fun! They don't have to be realistic! We use many colors in our decorations, the more the better! And we don't even bother to match them because we feel they're more whimsical when they're colorful.

The best thing to do when coloring fondant is to work in small batches. This can be a messy process. We recommend wearing latex gloves if you do not want to get dye on your hands.

Start with a 5-inch ball of fondant and knead it in your hands a bit. It will become pliable and ready to roll or mold into whatever shape you desire. It is at this time we add the dye.

We use gel paste as opposed to liquid food coloring to dye our fondant. Gel paste is very concentrated so you need very little to get good colored fondant. Start with 2 small drops and knead. Add more coloring to achieve the desired color.

*When making colored fondant, use color sparingly at first. It's always easier to add color than to take it away!*

Kneading warms fondant and incorporates the added color.

Remember, it is always easier to add more color. If the color becomes too dark, take a bit of the colored fondant and add that to a larger piece of white fondant. Don't add white to the large colored piece or you will create a lot of wasted fondant.

Dying dark colors requires quite a bit of gel paste kneaded into the fondant. We find that black and purple dyes leave a bit of an aftertaste, so we try use chocolate fondant instead.

If your project requires many colors of fondant, we suggest making all of the batches of colors at one time. That way, you do not have to stop and start in the midst of creating the cookies. It's like having all of your ingredients ready before preparing a meal.

There are two ways to blend colors of fondant:
• Drop dots of two colors of gel paste into the fondant and mix until you achieve your desired color. Ex: blue + yellow = green.
• Use an equal part of already rolled blue fondant with already rolled yellow and knead it together. Voila! It's green!

Part of the fun is seeing the colors you can create. We work basically with the same palette of colors—soft pinks, greens, blues, yellows, etc. We also use bright tones of these colors. We stay away from colors like maroon or royal blue because they do not seem as appetizing!

Make sure you store the colors in separate airtight baggies.

## PATTERNED FONDANT

It's also fun to make designs in fondant as you roll it. Some ideas for creating designs include:

### Dots

Let's say you want blue dots on pink fondant. First, make blue fondant. Then make pink fondant. Roll the pink fondant until it is a bit thicker than you want. Make pea-sized balls of blue fondant with your hands. Place the balls on the pink fondant and roll again. Roll in different ways so the dots don't totally lose their shape. Your dots will incorporate into the main piece of fondant, creating pink fondant with blue dots!

### Lines

Lines are created in the fondant the same way as dots. Instead of rolling pea-size balls of fondant, roll thin, snake-like ropes and place them on a rolled piece of fondant.

Cross snakes to make zig zags and use different colors to make plaids.

### Striation

We use a lot of color striation. The cookies don't look as flat and they seem to have more depth and interest. By just kneading white fondant into any bit of colored fondant, various patters will appear. You can roll the fondant at this point and see what designs you create!

Keep in mind that fondant can turn murky from rolling contrasting color combinations together. Try to use colors that, when combined, will create another color. Ex: Blue dots on pink base kneaded together will turn purple.

Roll fondant dots in all ways so they don't lose their shape.

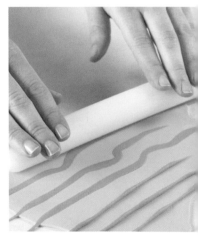

Rolling lines into the fondant.

# Meringue Powder Royal Icing

*Traditionally, royal icing is made using egg whites.*
*However, this can be unsafe since the egg whites are uncooked.*
*Royal icing made with meringue powder does away with this concern.*

———◆———

## WHAT YOU NEED:

¼ cup meringue powder
½ cup cold water
1 pound 10x powdered sugar

## DIRECTIONS:

Add meringue powder to cold water in a mixing bowl. Beat on medium speed until you see soft peaks (2 to 3 minutes). Add sugar, one cup at a time, beating the mixture after each cup. Beat for a total time of 5 to 7 minutes.

Store in an airtight container until ready to use.

# Piping

● **Margie says:** When I have an order of many cookies and have to pipe repeatedly, I go into what Abbey calls the "Piping zone." A rhythm develops and the movement of my hand results in an even flow along the cookies. Swirls are almost musical, like lines waltzing across the pan of cookies. Dots are like little staccato notes that jump across the cookies!

Piping must be relaxed. Allow your hand to dance across the cookies. Before you pipe onto cookies, practice piping lines and dots onto parchment paper. Try angling the pastry bag in different ways to see how different line widths can be formed. Draw lots of lines randomly and just let your hand follow the lines with the piping bag.

When I first began the use the piping bag, I was nervous about making mistakes. So I only used white icing. I could always "erase"

*Angle your pastry bag in different ways to create different lines.*

it if necessary. White is a lot more forgiving than other colors, which makes it a good practice color. When it's still wet, you can just wipe the icing off. If you make a mistake with other colors, it is best to totally let them dry and then pick it off gently with a toothpick. Then proceed back over the same line.

You can find pastry bags and tips at your local grocery store, specialty cooking stores, or craft stores.

When you're ready to pipe, fill the pastry bag only half-way, as a full bag will result in icing coming out of the top of the bag and making a mess. Release any air from the top of your pastry bag before twisting it at the top to keep icing from spilling out. Hold the bag in your writing hand and guide it with your other hand.

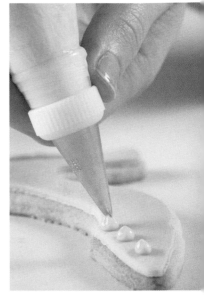

*For full dots, hold the bag for a bit as you pipe.*

# Suppliers

• **AMERICAN BAKELS** is a wonderful provider of fondant and fondant decorations. They can be found online at www.americanbakels.com.

• **PFEIL AND HOLING** is a great resource for decorating materials. They sell a variety of novelty cake decorations, gel paste, sugar flowers, meringue powder, pearl dust, molded sugar decorations, pastry bags, bakery supplies, pans and utensils. They are online at www.cakedeco.com.

• **KITCHEN COLLECTABLES** has a large collection of copper cookie cutters and baking and decorating supplies. They are online at www.kitchengifts.com.

• **SUGAR CRAFT** has a wide variety of decorating supplies, fondant tools and cutters, and packaging materials. They are also a great place to buy textured rolling pins. They are online at www.sugarcraft.com.

• And if you're in the neighborhood, **THE FLOUR POT** sells and ships supplies nationwide, including gel paste, fondant pins, fondant, meringue powder, cookie cutters. Find us online at www.flourpotcookies.com.

# Conversion Tables

## METRIC EQUIVALENTS FOR VOLUME

| U.S. | Imperial | Metric |
|------|----------|--------|
| ⅛ tsp. | — | 0.6 ml |
| ½ tsp. | — | 2.5 ml |
| ¾ tsp. | — | 4.0 ml |
| 1 tsp. | — | 5.0 ml |
| 1½ tsp. | — | 7.0 ml |
| 2 tsp. | — | 10.0 ml |
| 3 tsp. | — | 15.0 ml |
| 4 tsp. | — | 20.0 ml |
| 1 Tbsp. | — | 15.0 ml |
| 1½ Tbsp. | — | 22.0 ml |
| 2 Tbsp. (⅛ cup) | 1 fl. oz | 30.0 ml |
| 2½ Tbsp. | — | 37.0 ml |
| 3 Tbsp. | — | 44.0 ml |
| ⅓ cup | — | 57.0 ml |
| 4 Tbsp. (¼ cup) | 2 fl. oz | 59.0 ml |
| 5 Tbsp. | — | 74.0 ml |
| 6 Tbsp. | — | 89.0 ml |
| 8 Tbsp. (½ cup) | 4 fl. oz | 120.0 ml |
| ¾ cup | 6 fl. oz | 178.0 ml |
| 1 cup | 8 fl. oz | 237.0 ml (.24 liters) |
| 1½ cups | — | 354.0 ml |
| 1¾ cups | — | 414.0 ml |
| 2 cups (1 pint) | 16 fl. oz | 473.0 ml |
| 4 cups (1 quart) | 32 fl. oz | (.95 liters) |
| 5 cups | — | (1.183 liters) |
| 16 cups (1 gallon) | 128 fl. oz | (3.8 liters) |

## GENERIC FORMULAS FOR METRIC CONVERSION

| | |
|---|---|
| Ounces to grams | multiply ounces by 28.35 |
| Pounds to grams | multiply pounds by 453.5 |
| Cups to liters | multiply cups by .24 |
| Fahrenheit to Centigrade | subtract 32 from Fahrenheit, multiply by five and divide by 9 |

## OVEN TEMPERATURES

| Degrees Fahrenheit | Degrees Centigrade | British Gas Marks |
|--------------------|--------------------|-------------------|
| 200° | 93° | — |
| 250° | 120° | — |
| 275° | 140° | 1 |
| 300° | 150° | 2 |
| 325° | 165° | 3 |
| 350° | 175° | 4 |
| 375° | 190° | 5 |
| 400° | 200° | 6 |
| 450° | 230° | 8 |

## METRIC EQUIVALENTS FOR WEIGHT

| U.S. | Metric |
|---|---|
| 1 oz | 28 g |
| 2 oz | 58 g |
| 3 oz | 85 g |
| 4 oz (¼ lb.) | 113 g |
| 5 oz | 142 g |
| 6 oz | 170 g |
| 7 oz | 199 g |
| 8 oz (½ lb.) | 227 g |
| 10 oz | 284 g |
| 12 oz (¾ lb.) | 340 g |
| 14 oz | 397 g |
| 16 oz (1 lb.) | 454 g |

## METRIC EQUIVALENTS FOR BUTTER

| U.S. | Metric |
|---|---|
| 2 tsp. | 10.0 g |
| 1 Tbsp. | 15.0 g |
| 1½ Tbsp. | 22.5 g |
| 2 Tbsp. (1 oz) | 55.0 g |
| 3 Tbsp. | 70.0 g |
| ¼ lb. (1 stick) | 110.0 g |
| ½ lb. (2 sticks) | 220.0 g |

## METRIC EQUIVALENTS FOR LENGTH (USE ALSO FOR PAN SIZES)

| U.S. | Metric |
|---|---|
| ¼ inch | .65 cm |
| ½ inch | 1.25 cm |
| 1 inch | 2.50 cm |
| 2 inches | 5.00 cm |
| 3 inches | 6.00 cm |
| 4 inches | 8.00 cm |
| 5 inches | 11.00 cm |
| 6 inches | 15.00 cm |
| 7 inches | 18.00 cm |
| 8 inches | 20.00 cm |
| 9 inches | 23.00 cm |
| 12 inches | 30.50 cm |
| 15 inches | 38.00 cm |